RECRUIT R!GHT

Every Employers Comprehensive Guide to Foolproof Hiring!

RECRUIT R!GHT

SHEFALI TRIPATHI

Leading Recruitment Strategist
Director of India's 5000 Best MSME nominated Company

Published Internationally by

Pendown Press

Powered by G Gullybaba.com

PENDOWN PRESS

Powered by **Gullybaba Publishing House Pvt. Ltd.,**
An ISO 9001 & ISO 14001 Certified Co.,
Regd. Office: 2525/193, 1st Floor, Onkar Nagar-A, Tri Nagar,
Delhi-110035
Ph.: 09350849407, 09312235086
E-mail: info@pendownpress.com
Branch Office: 1A/2A, 20, Hari Sadan, Ansari Road,
Daryaganj, New Delhi-110002
Ph.: 011-45794768
Website: PendownPress.com

First Edition: 2021
Price: ₹179/-
ISBN: 978-93-90479-19-1

Layout Design: Pendown Press Publishing

Printed and bound in India by Thomson Press India Ltd.

TESTIMONIALS

"I know Shefali for more than 15 years now and have worked with her closely. Along with her team, Shefali handled a mass recruitment project efficiently and assisted us in building a powerful team. Her ability to understand the requirement and locate the best match makes her an exceptionally talented recruiter. She is honest, dedicated, prompt, and reliable. I have not seen many professionals in this domain with such command over their work. She never fails to deliver; I strongly recommend her."

–Mr. Aditya Goyal

"Shefali has been handling our recruitment needs for the last many years. She is prompt, methodical, and strategic in her approach & helped us every time we needed a good resource."

–Mr. Vikrant Rai

"Under Shefali's leadership, Career Genii has always helped and guided us as a boutique recruitment firm in the domain of Luxury Retail and Exports of Textile and Lifestyle. Shefali's capability to listen, understand, and make her team execute is something we always depend upon. This support is unmatched."

–Mr. Karan Pahwa

"I have known Shefali professionally and personally as well. She is a happy go lucky person who is also an excellent professional when it comes to working. Her understanding of what is required is very good and so is the delivery. I find her honest, dedicated, and very helpful which are the key requirements for building a good professional relationship. I recommend Shefali for her services and support."

–Mr. Anil Jain

CONTENTS

My Journey

{Page: i}

The Big Questions

{Page: v}

Strategy 1
Explore Your Goldmine

{Page: 1}

Strategy 2
Build Your Database

{Page: 2}

Strategy 3
Become A Preferred Employer

{Page: 3}

Strategy 4
Create a detailed Job Description and Key Result Area

{Page: 4}

Strategy 5
Use Social Media as an Effective Hiring Tool

{Page: 6}

Strategy 6
Consider Hiring a Third-Party Firm

{Page: 7}

Strategy 7
Plan For Engaging And Pleasing Interactions

{Page: 8}

Strategy 8
Choose wisely

{Page: 9}

Strategy 9
Negotiate a Win-Win Deal

{Page: 10}

Strategy 10
Establish Simple Processes in Place

{Page: 11}

Conclusion

{Page: 13}

What is the 'Recruit Right Framework'?

{Page:15}

Success Stories

{Page:20}

Make Your Move, Now

{Page:22}

What's Next?

{Page:23}

What do senior industry professionals think of us

{Page:25}

MY JOURNEY

While Steve Jobs played a crucial role in creating Apple, it is the team who played an equally vital role. It does not make sense to hire people and tell them what to do. Instead, we hire smart people so that they can tell us what to do.

A well-planned recruitment strategy can work wonders for your business if put together seamlessly. It is possible to **build high-performance teams and** Turbocharge your business by recruiting, retaining and nurturing A-level teams that have the same entrepreneurial mindset as you do.

Trust me as I talk from experience...

Hello, my name is Shefali Tripathi. I am a Recruitment Strategist and Creator of The Recruit Right Framework. I represent Career Genii Consulting Private Limited, a boutique strategic recruitment organization for the Domain of garment and textile manufacturers in India and APAC countries based out of New Delhi, India.

My tryst with the amazing world of Garment and Textile started in 1993 when I was still in school. I was so fascinated that

I decided to pursue my Post Graduation (D) in this field from one of the most eminent design institutes, Pearl Academy in New Delhi. Strict timelines of the Garment and Textile Industry were challenging. After working for a substantial amount of time, I was soon selected by an international fashion institute as a faculty where recruitment of graduating students came as an additional responsibility. I had confusion all over. Students waiting for hours to be interviewed, answering irrelevant questions from HR, and filling endless forms seemed to solve no immediate purpose. Something was amiss. That was when I developed a deep interest in recruitments and understood the recruitment struggle. It was tough for professionals to find suitable jobs and businesses to build performing teams. Career Genii was conceptualized in 2002 to solve this problem.

I wanted to help MSMEs increase profits by building successful teams. In the next few years, I noticed that despite organizations employing candidates seemingly suitable, they struggled to grow. Leaders and business owners were still fighting over petty operational issues. Despite the teams available, they were not doing what they should be or focusing on building business further.

I confidently concluded that recruitments alone would not solve the problem related to operations and business growth. Something was missing.

I am now on a journey to help employers identify why, when, where and how to build a powerful business by finding High- Performance Teams that not only deliver, but also work for your firm for longer tenures saving you the exercise of hiring time and again. Employees love People-oriented companies and they prosper more than others because the business owners can focus on building the business.

Career Genii has helped organizations in India and APAC countries to build their business by way of hiring and retaining high performing teams. It has been an enriching journey where I have been on a mission to help employers find associates who work with a sense of ownership and free up their time. Having catered to more than 1,000 firms, Career Genii, today, stands tall as a leader helping our business partners RECRUIT RIGHT! Today, we have business associations with Manufacturing firms, E- commerce firms, Retail brands and labels, Institutions, buying and liaison firms, inspection companies and expanding.

My journey so far has been brilliant!

You must be wondering why I am talking about my journey with you. What is the purpose of information shared in the following pages? Here's why:

- One, being in love with Recruit Right, it breaks my heart to see how business owners and leaders suffer day in and day out with a never-ending struggle of building powerful teams. It saddens me to see how employers are still struggling with simple issues that can be solved by strategic thinking, planning and executing a Methodical Approach.

  So, I want to put maximum Employers and their Human Resource Team on the path of finding the right talent with a minimum investment of time, effort and money and build lasting teams that contribute towards your business growth.

- Two, it is next to impossible to coach everyone personally due to time and geographical constraints, so this book is my offering to all those employers, employees and organizations who/that can learn from my journey and experiences as a Strategic Recruiter and Trainer. If you use the strategies contained within, you can make a real killing and grow your business by hiring a growth-oriented focused team. In my experience, such professionals are hard to find and tough to build teams that will turbocharge your business. Let me share the strategies that will get you the dream team that not only works with ownership, but also cares for the growth of your business. I hope these sharing of my experiences will guide you to the path of success and excellence.

As a leader of your firm, your task is to build the business and take your organization forward instead of getting stuck in issues that can be resolved by strategic planning and execution. Most of my clients had no choice but to take things into their hands and get into recruitments directly because they were unaware of the scientific approach. After implementing the suggestions given herewith, they have not only freed-up their time, but also do not suffer from challenges related to building teams.

Just like other aspects of businesses like marketing, operations, design, production, quality, planning and other departments, recruitment requires strategic planning and execution. You will attract, recruit, retain and nurture right talent in your organization that will smoothly run all the other departments seamlessly so that you can focus on business growth.

THE BIG QUESTIONS

Do you have your A-level team ready for THE BIG LEAP or:

1. Are you still tolerating employees who repeatedly make mistakes costing you money and goodwill?

2. As the owner of your enterprise, are you still working 80+ hours every week to cover-up for your employees?

3. Do you feel that your team is just filling up space and not helping you make more money?

4. Are you finding yourself spending precious time in endless hiring and losing focus on growing your business?

An ace warrior needs a capable team of soldiers to win a war. As a business owner or CEO, you have plenty of opportunities to grow but need a winning team by your side to make it happen. You will need A-grade players who eagerly solve problems, create strategies, produce excellent results, take great care of your clients, and take work off your plate.

My Recruit Right Framework makes this possible for you! What is it? And how it helps you to see the higher ground in the war for talent?

From my experience, here are a few strategies and learnings to attract a steady team of top-notch applicants waiting to work for you.

STRATEGY 1

EXPLORE YOUR GOLDMINE

The easiest hack is to look into your firm. The reason you have reached so far is because of a few good decisions taken where people stood by you through the tough times over the years. These people understand you and your business better than others. They are tried, tested, and with comparatively less training will save you the exercise of recruiting, training, and inducting new talent. Pay attention to your current employees and see who has the talent waiting to be groomed. If they are your well-wishers, they will prove to be an asset and be accountable for the work entrusted to them.

STRATEGY 2

BUILD YOUR DATABASE

Build a database of prospective employees for your organization. Encourage employee referrals and offer incentives against successful recruitments. Good employees will not hesitate to go out of their way to locate people in their professional circle to help you hire the right talent. An organization must remain in the hunt for right talent throughout the year. Save a good resume' for future consideration. It can prove to be an asset 6 to 12 months down the line after the candidate has built the required skill you are looking for. Save soft copies of these documents for later use. Systems can be built to save vital documents and important information related to every professional who is hired or rejected for future reference.

BECOME
A PREFERRED EMPLOYER

Your team is like your sales force; it constantly works towards building your goodwill. Happy professionals speak highly of you and promote you even after leaving the company. It should be your top agenda to address and constructively resolve conflicts to create a happy workforce. Unhappy employees cost goodwill and adversely affect your business in the long run.

Work on your image to attract right talent to build a ready database of employable skill. Share stories and experiences of your employees on social media and website, small videos of the office activities with happy employees, blogs on employee experiences, etc. Mention the links of these blogs on your website. This will position you as a positive, and preferred employer.

CREATE A DETAILED JOB DESCRIPTION AND KEY RESULT AREA

Like you would carefully curate an advertisement to sell your products or services, the same importance has to be given to the Job Description (JD) for an open mandate. A good JD is a single point of reference when it comes to delivery, execution and achievement of key results. The Key Result Area (KRA) defines an employee's job position and duty. It also refers to different areas of work for which the employees may take responsibility. KRA focuses on the JD (Job Description) of the workers.

To get the maximum out of current resources available, you should exactly know how you want your employees to plan their working day. They must be aware of the roles, responsibilities and timelines associated with their work. Recognize and identify tools that can help your employees organize and operate methodically instead of delivering random duties. Encourage them to utilise free online tools to plan their day, week, month the year ahead.

USE SOCIAL MEDIA AS AN EFFECTIVE HIRING TOOL

Does it matter who is reading your job advertisement? The effectiveness of the message is only when it reaches prospective candidates. Industry-specific groups on LinkedIn, Facebook, WhatsApp are popular and a perfect platform to post your requirements. Once a carefully curated professional message is shared, such platforms also help in brand-building. Visibility encourages people to explore more about your company, current employees and work culture.

STRATEGY 6

CONSIDER HIRING A THIRD-PARTY FIRM

Engaging an industry-specific recruitment service provider who has delivered a few assignments in similar domain to save your time and effort. Recruiters work closely with job seekers and understand their needs better. Professionals feel free to openly discuss their preferences and past experiences that help them make the right choice. Choose a recruiter with a high work ethic and a history of serving good organizations. Cross-verify the details with a common source to ensure suitability. Encourage the recruiter to ask questions regarding the JD or the company for more clarity.

STRATEGY 7

PLAN FOR ENGAGING AND PLEASING INTERACTIONS

Treat prospective employees like prospective customers. Show concern and value for their time. Plan to create a smooth, painless and comfortable interview process showing your care and concern. For the applicant, it is a window to the organisation's work environment. Choose not to keep the candidates waiting and conduct the interview as soon as possible. Structured interviews keep you on the defined path and reach a transparent, clear outcome by the end of an interaction. You may choose to conduct a technical test immediately after completing the required rounds of interviews instead of requesting another appointment.

STRATEGY 8

CHOOSE WISELY

Confident professionals are often considered a good resource. You will be tempted to extend an offer immediately. Do not get carried away by the confidence of a professional but choose a person owning a good character. Confidence depends upon knowledge of a product or job that can be built by training. As competence increases, the level of confidence improves. The character will decide if the candidate will be an asset to your organization or burn a hole in your pocket. Invest a few hundred in conducting employee verification and referencing. Secure your business by hiring a person of good character.

STRATEGY 9

NEGOTIATE
A WIN-WIN DEAL

It is common among employers to negotiate salary down to the lowest possible. Professionals pick up an opportunity at a compromised salary because they are desperate to join. It is obvious that such professionals will not hesitate to switch upon being offered a better salary. Create a salary breakup with a fixed and a variable component that is paid depending upon the performance and profits. This has often been a win-win for both the employer and employee. In my opinion, employers are happy to share profits with growth oriented employees. Have clear, visible and achievable time-based goals that seem motivating to employees.

STRATEGY 10

ESTABLISH SIMPLE PROCESSES IN PLACE

Like other departments, recruitments need a methodical approach to make it a success. Below are simple indicators to conduct shortlisting and Recruit Right.

A. Resume' Analysis

- Check for current residence and if it is well connected to your office location.

- The minimum average Tenure of 2 years with every employer.

- Look for unexplained Gaps and seek clarification.

- Pay attention to Technical and additional qualifications.

- Analyse written communication skills.

B. Telephonic Interview

- Verify details on the resumes.

- Check reasons for job changes.

- Seek explanation for gaps in the Resume'.

- Overview of Technical Understanding of the role.

- Observe verbal communication skills.

C. Personal Interaction

- Conduct technical/practical assessment if needed.

- Gauge integrity and other crucial values.

- Check fitment to your work culture.

- Analyse overall personality and mannerisms.

- Observe non-verbal communication.

D. Joining formalities

- Issue offer and appointment letter with terms.

- Get the documents signed by the employee.

- Ask for identity proof and photograph for records.

- Collect Experience documents and letters.

- Verify Salary by seeking proof or ask for bank certificates.

E. Employee Verification

- Create a format to conduct employee verification.

- Verify employee conduct with at least two past employers.

- Seek inputs from immediate Supervisors or Directors.

- If the role demands, verify conduct from vendors or clients.

CONCLUSION

Like many other business decisions and processes, recruitments are also tricky but an equally or more important part of your business. A little consideration, compassion and careful planning can easily establish you as a preferred employer, attracting the right talent and building a ready- to-use database.

Let us together create a growth-oriented hub of talented professionals who are happy, content and feel lucky to be a part of your company.

You have two choices:

1. **Boutique Strategic Recruitment Services**

   I have been a recruitment strategist for almost two decades now, helping organizations in India and APAC countries. Finding talent suiting the requirement of organizations engaged in the businesses of manufacturing, exports, retail, e-commerce, buying in India, APAC countries and Africa has been my biggest strength. I also recruit Indian, Sri Lankan and Bangladesh nationals.

Through writing this book and various articles for magazines on HR and recruitment challenges, I have over the years become an expert who can help you build high- performance teams. You can Turbocharge your performance by recruiting, retaining and nurturing A- level teams that have the same entrepreneurial mindset as you do.

2. **Use The Recruit Right Framework specially created to help you multiply growth that has been developed based on the above 10 Strategies.**

    The Recruit Right Framework offers an ideal solution to recruitment woes for all organizations regardless of their turnover, Number of employees, Industry or location on the globe. Decision- makers at all levels can learn the secrets of Recruiting Right and successfully implement the framework. Top management executives, HR professionals or department heads involved in the recruitment process can quickly escalate growth by building the capability to Recruit Right. Recruitment is a scientific approach and requires an in-depth understanding of the exact requirement and Key Result Areas associated with it.

WHAT IS THE 'RECRUIT RIGHT FRAMEWORK'?

How it helps you seize the high-ground in the war for talent? Allow me to devise your recruitment process flow and train you into becoming Master Recruiters. This extensive and powerful program is changing lives. Take advantage and stop bleeding your resources.

Recruit Right Framework is a revolutionary approach that has helped clients build high-performance teams making rapid growth in the shortest time in any industry or economy.

Here is the three-step process of Recruit Right Framework to get exponential growth:

1. **Recruit Right:** Strategies to attract a steady stream of top-notch applicants waiting to work for you.

2. **Retain Right:** Tools to become the best employer by providing your team a great place to work and growth opportunities.

3. **Nurture Right:** A foolproof process to build the next line of leaders ready to take your business to a new high.

After applying this system you are guaranteed to...

- Reach and maintain a flow of high-quality candidates on demand.

- Retain your ninja team by providing a workplace that is pleasurable and productive.

- Nurture your team to build a pool of high-performing future leaders. Generate high growth and get an exponential increase in profits.

And finally

- Take a dream vacation to celebrate this accomplishment without worrying about who will run the show in your absence.

Over 85% of companies struggle in hiring a ninja team. 99.3% of my clients don't!

Let me share a few Testimonials:

"Using the Recruit Right techniques, I could save my HR cost of no less than 2CR. I can now foresee 10X growth by way of building a team that shares my vision."

–Ms Kirti Saluja

"She had given me a strategy and I hired 10 top-level team members in a breeze. I can't believe how much easier hiring could be that too in a record time."

–Mr Rohit Kapoor

"With a high-performing team in place, our revenue has doubled! I chose to implement the strategies Shefali shared and got astonishing results!"

–Mr Prayag Singh Thakur

"We are a growing company and the single largest hindrance in our growth was the ability to recruit Right People at the Right Time. We hired multiple consultants in the past without desired outcome. The RECRUIT RIGHT PROGRAM has been transformational for us. After implementing the strategies proposed, we now have a continuous stream of desired professionals available at our end. Our sincere thanks to Shefali Tripathi for creating such a powerful and simple to implement framework. We now have a robust hiring mechanism."

–Archit Srivastava

I am honored to have helped more than 750 companies in India and overseas. I have enabled them to eliminate the stress and strain of recruiting the right people, nurture them, and retain them to grow exponentially. Whether it is your first hire or the 200th, my unconventional approach is a crucial step in transforming your business into a highly profitable venture. For how long will you tolerate burning your hard-earned money and never-to-come-back time experimenting with old school HR systems? In today's hyper-competitive market, old school HR systems do not work. What would really work for you is a revolutionary approach to strategic hiring and actively cultivating top talents. More than ever, hiring and nurturing the best people requires foresight, planning, alertness, and decisive action. With the "Recruit Right Framework", you have everything you need to seize the high-ground in the war for talent and maintain it for long-term growth.

Discover the secrets to solve your number one challenge and solve your hiring challenges using a realistic, attainable approach.

Connect with me immediately to learn how best to integrate this system with your company. For the miraculous results that I have produced, I am popularly known as the HR queen in the industry.

Discover how 750+ entrepreneurs just like you generate a combined $ 200 million profit through the "Recruit Right Framework" and how best this can be applied in the company. Schedule a discovery call with me to solve your years of HR challenges in just 30 minutes.

"Listen to what Shefali has to say. This gentlewoman solved my 30 years of HR challenges in 30-minutes."

–Rohit Khurrana

Reach me at 9811410172 or shefali@careergenii.com to understand how I can help you and your organization hire the resource you have been looking for and streamline your entire recruitment system.

Once you get associated with me, you will realize:

1. It is basically about understanding the problem area and finding a long-term permanent solution.

2. You can stop burning a hole in your pocket immediately by getting in touch with an expert who can resolve all your pain points.

3. There is no need to keep reviewing multiple resumes coming from multiple sources and investing hours in conducting interviews instead of focusing on business growth.

Choose us to be your extended arm that is genuinely interested in the growth of your company.

With experience, I have learned what not to do and what doesn't work. I have worked with the best organizations in India and overseas. There is a proven formula that works with rapid results. It is possible to locate the right resource in the minimum amount of time and effort put by your HR and the management of the company by building the right system. With my technical expertise acquired over two decades clubbed with my understanding of Human Psychology, I help my clients reach their goal flawlessly.

Unlike the age-old rusted conventional approach, my approach is radically different, which helps you reach the right desired outcome.

Let's do this together...

I am not only supporting organizations and helping them grow, but also playing a vital role in multiple women's lives by creating an all-women organization where we train and empower them. This gives me a sense of fulfilment and pride also because the Government of India has nominated Career Genii Consulting Pvt Ltd for India's 5000 Best MSMEs award for the year 2020.

I am on a dual mission to not only help organizations by making them independent of this vicious cycle of conducting endless searches but also make them self-sufficient. You won't need a recruiter after implementing what I offer.

SUCCESS STORIES

1. An American label of high-fashion garments wanted to establish its manufacturing base in New Delhi. After implementing the Recruit Right Framework, the firm has ever-since been hiring directly and is free of all recruitment woes. They have a ready database of good quality professionals to hire from as and when required.

2. A project was executed in Ranchi where a multi-branded well-established retail chain was facing multiple issues with their sourcing and delivery teams. They were looking for a long-term solution. The entire team was re-built, and Recruit Right Framework was installed after identifying the challenges. The retail firm has now become self-sufficient in handling their work force needs.

3. A US-based organization of promotional goods for international brands wanted to start India operations. They were desperately on the lookout for somebody who could not only help them with creating recruitment systems but also bring in the right team who understood functionalities related to the product, process flow,

sourcing from China. Career Genii not only built the team from scratch, but also later implemented the recruit Right Framework for long term success. The company's turnover has multiplied and the money is being invested in the right direction.

4. A textile manufacturing firm in Bangladesh expressed grave concerns over attrition of professionals. After restructuring their recruitment operations, the company has regularly been hiring from India and Sri Lanka.

5. An Indian-owned China-based buying house exporting to the US was planning expansion. We were given the responsibility to build a team of Indians. After carefully implementing the Recruit Right Framework, four professionals were hired within 21 days and the firm became completely independent of recruiters, saving millions of rupees.

MAKE YOUR MOVE, NOW

MAKE YOUR MOVE, NOW If you have been wasting precious time, effort and money chasing multiple consultants without fruitful results, then perhaps it is time you stop burning the midnight oil. Look at solutions I offer to achieve freedom from recruitment woes. It is my ultimate goal to help you believe in the possibility of locating the right talent at the right time and price all by yourself. All you need is to implement my ultimate Recruit Right Framework.

WHAT'S NEXT?

Join my Free Masterclass to experience the power of Recruit Right Framework LIVE! During this popular 90-minute Masterclass, you will deep-dive into the time-tested system of hiring, retaining, and nurturing a great team. Register here:

"The masterclass is worth lakhs of rupees and Shefali is offering it for free. What an amazing service she is offering to the business community!"

–Girrish Mehtani

"These 90 minutes are like learning of a lifetime. I feel so stupid of myself overlooking such basic things while recruiting the people earlier."

–Ronak Gupta

Book a strategy call with me by sending a message at +91 9811410172. You can also drop me an email at shefali@ careergenii.com.

Scan below to view my LinkedIn Page for more information:

WHAT DO SENIOR INDUSTRY PROFESSIONALS THINK OF US

"My relationship with Career Genii and Shefali has been unique. Many years ago, I approached them as a job seeker and they helped me in every possible way to crack the opportunity. Working with them is just not about getting a job but it's like a complete package to ensure that you make it till the end. I today work as Shefali's client and highly recommend her services. ST and her team are ethical, sincere, honest and undoubtedly the masters of the trade. I have never been disappointed even when it comes to the toughest positions to work on. They are professional and understand the value of time. I also recommend Shefali and Career Genii for their commitment, dedication, and sincerity which is rare to find."

–Kokila Lakra

"*Shefali has been an Ace when it comes to interviewing skills and strategies about cracking great opportunities. Her well-researched and methodical approach always works. She has aided me in garnering several professional opportunities and has helped me reach a remarkable place in my career. She gives in her 100% for every client and her support is commendable. I highly recommend her.*"

–Ms. Shyamlee Khanna

"*I have worked with Shefali closely who got me the opportunities most suited to my profile. As a recruiter, her guidance on resume' and interview skills are really helpful. I see her as an expert of Recruitment strategies who always ensures that we hire a team of extraordinary employees as and when required. I recommend her highly and endorse her skills as a trainer and recruiter. Thanks, Shefali... you are a wonderful person.*"

–Ms. Ekta Sabharwal

"*I have known Shefali for almost 10 years now. Shefali understands and perceives the pulse of the business in-depth. She has unique and effective strategies thus becoming a leader in the recruitment industry.*"

–Shailesh Gurnan

Notes:

____

____

____

____

____

____

____

____

____

____

____

____

____

____

Reach me now:

📞 +91 9811410172 ✉ shefali@careergenii.com

Notes:

Reach me now:

📞 +91 9811410172 ✉ shefali@careergenii.com

Notes:

Reach me now:

📞 +91 9811410172 ✉ shefali@careergenii.com

www.ingramcontent.com/pod-product-compliance
Lightning Source LLC
Chambersburg PA
CBHW031004180726
47993CB00018B/1557